COOL JOBS

for Super Sales Kids

Ways to Make Money Selling Stuff

Pam Scheunemann

ABDO
Publishing Company

Visit us at www.abdopublishing.com

Published by ABDO Publishing Company, 8000 West 78th Street, Edina, Minnesota 55439.
Copyright © 2011 by Abdo Consulting Group, Inc. International copyrights reserved in all countries.
No part of this book may be reproduced in any form without written permission from the publisher.
The Checkerboard Library™ is a trademark and logo of ABDO Publishing Company.

Printed in the United States , North Mankato, Minnesota
052010
092010

 PRINTED ON RECYCLED PAPER

Design and Production: Kelly Doudna, Mighty Media, Inc.
Series Editor: Liz Salzmann
Photo Credits: Kelly Doudna, iStockPhoto (Jim Jurica),
Shutterstock
Money Savvy Pig® photo courtesy of Money Savvy
Generation/www.msgen.com

**Library of Congress
Cataloging-in-Publication Data**

Scheunemann, Pam, 1955-
  Cool jobs for super sales kids : ways to make money selling
stuff / Pam Scheunemann.
    p. cm. -- (Cool kid jobs)
  Includes index.
  ISBN 978-1-61613-197-5
  1. Money-making projects for children--Juvenile literature. 2.
Selling--Juvenile literature. I. Title.
  HF5392.S34 2011
  658.85--dc22
                        2010004315

NOTE TO ADULTS

A job can be a good learning experience for you and your child. Be sure to encourage your child to discuss his or her job ideas with you. Talk about the risks and the benefits. Set up some rules for your child's safety with regard to:

* working with strangers

* transportation to and from the job

* proper and safe use of tools or equipment

* giving out phone numbers or e-mail addresses

* emergency contacts

Contents

Why Sell Things?

There are a lot of reasons to sell things. The first one you probably think of is to earn money. But you can get more out of sales than just money. You can learn new skills, meet new people, and get some experience.

MAKING MONEY

When you sell things, keep in mind what they cost you. You should sell them for more than you paid. Otherwise you won't make any money. Don't forget to charge a little extra for your time!

BESIDES MONEY

You will gain more than money when you sell things. You also get experience and learn about being responsible. That means planning carefully, charging fair prices, and being respectful to people.

Volunteering is doing a job you don't get paid for. But you can earn other rewards. You can learn new skills that will help you get other jobs. And you can feel good about helping out!

What Can You Do with Your Money?

There are four things you can do with the money you earn.

SAVE

Saving is keeping your money in a safe place. You add money a little at a time as you earn it. Soon you could save enough for something such as a new bike.

SPEND

Spending is using your money to buy things you want. Maybe you want to go to a movie or buy a new computer game.

DONATE

It is important to give some of your earnings to organizations that help others.

INVEST

Investing is saving for long-term goals such as college expenses.

Ask your parents to help you decide how much money to use for each purpose. You'll be glad you did!

Money Savvy Pig®

What's Your Plan?

Planning is very important if you want to make money selling stuff. Poor planning can cause you to lose money. Ask yourself the following questions.

WHAT WILL YOU SELL?

What's your product? Maybe it's something you can grow or make. Do you like to garden? Are you an artist? Maybe you can bake really well. You could also buy things and resell them. You will be most successful if you sell something you know about. If you want to try something new, learn about it first. Look all around you for ideas. Try the library or look online.

WHO ARE YOUR CUSTOMERS?

Who will buy your product? Market **research** can help you figure this out. You need to consider these questions about your market.

Is it a good product? Make or buy a sample of the product. Show it to your friends, relatives, and neighbors. Ask if they think it's something people will want to buy. If they say yes, start out small. Get a few and try to sell them. If they sell quickly, make or buy more. If no one buys your samples, try something else.

Who wants or needs your product? Is it for men, women, teens, or younger kids? Is it for people with certain interests, such as sports or gardening?

Who is your competition? Are other people selling a similar product? If there are, how much do they charge? Why would people buy your product instead of the **competition's** product?

What is your product worth? How much do you think someone would pay for your product? Find out what other people or stores charge for similar products. Ask friends and relatives what they would pay for your product.

WHERE WILL YOU SELL YOUR PRODUCT?

Location. Location. Location! Finding a good place to sell your product is very important. Is there an event that will **attract** people who want your product? For example, if you are selling crafts, look for craft shows in your area. Or you could host a party to sell your product. Invite friends, neighbors, and relatives. Does your neighborhood have an annual **garage sale**? Try selling your product then.

WHEN WILL YOU SELL YOUR PRODUCT?

Timing is everything. Is your product something that people might buy any time? Or is it something that people only buy at certain times? For example, June is probably not a good time to sell something school related. But if you offer it in August or September, you will probably do pretty well. Or maybe your product would make a good gift. Right before the holidays would be a good time to try to sell it. Just use your common sense!

HOW WILL YOU SELL YOUR PRODUCT?

There are a lot of things you have to do to get started. It's a good idea to make a **schedule**. Include each task that needs to be done. Have you thought of everything you need to do? Think about having an adult around to give you advice.

If you are working with others, think about who will do each task. Make sure each person agrees on what they will be responsible for. Will you all have equal say or is there one person in charge? Talk through your plan. Hold meetings to talk about the progress of each task. If someone is behind, see if they need help to keep on schedule.

Great Goodies Schedul

Meetings will be held on Wednesday afternoons.

Date	What	Who
5-May	Make a sales plan	Bob and Bill
12-May	Get approval for location	Bill
12-May	Make signs/posters	Bill
12-May	Create expense/income budget	Bob
12-May	Research recipes	Bob
19-May	Purchase supplies	Bob and Bill
27-May	Make final preparations	Bob and Bill
27-May	Purchase cookies and ice	Bob and Bill
27-May	Package cookies	Bill
28-May	Put up arrow signs	Bill
28-May	Set up sales table/get out supplies	Bob and Bill
28-May	Make lemonade	Bob
29-May	SALE DAY 1	Bob and Bill
30-May	SALE DAY 2	Bob and Bill
31-May	SALE DAY 3	Bob and Bill
31-May	Put away supplies	Bob
31-May	Take down arrow signs	Bill
31-May	Fill out actual income and expenses to figure profit	Bob and Bill

Be Smart, Be Safe

Talk about your plans with your parents. Get their advice and permission. Find out if you need a permit to sell your product. Do you plan to sell food or drinks? Learn about local health and safety rules. An adult will need to oversee the preparation of any food products.

SALES SAFETY

In order to sell things, you will need to talk to strangers. Talk to your parents about how to interact with strangers. Never hold your sale alone. Have friends or an older brother or sister help out. A parent or other adult should be around during your sale. Set up in an area where there are a lot of people. Do not go up to people in cars to make a sale. Do not agree to bring your product to a customer's home.

Getting the Word Out

Okay, you've decided on a product. Now how do you let your customers know about it? There are different ways to get the word out.

BUSINESS CARDS

A simple business card can be very helpful in getting customers. Give cards to the people you talk to about your product. Maybe even give each person an extra so he or she can pass one along to a friend.

Your business card should have your name, your business name, and your phone number. Get permission from a parent before putting your home address, phone number, or e-mail address on a card.

WORD OF MOUTH

Let as many people know about your product as you can. They'll tell other people, and those people will tell more people, and so on.

Make Your Own Business Cards

PRO TIP
Use the computer to make your flyer and cards. Or, follow the steps here and on page 13 for a more personal touch.

1. On a piece of white paper, draw a rectangle with a black pen. It should be 3½ x 2 inches (9 x 5 cm). **Design** your business card inside the rectangle.

2. Make 11 copies of the card. Cut each one out, including the original. Cut outside the border so the lines show.

3. Tape the cards onto a piece of 8½ x 11-inch (22 x 28 cm) paper. Leave a ¼-inch (½ cm) border around the edge of the paper. This is your business card **master**.

4. Copy the master onto card stock. If you're using a black-and-white copier, try using colored card stock. Or, use white card stock and add color with markers or colored pencils.

5. Cut out your business cards. When you run out of cards, make more copies of your master.

WHAT YOU'LL NEED

white paper	tape
ruler	card stock (white or colored)
black pen	
copier	markers or colored pencils
scissors	

11

Fresh
Lemonade
&
Cookies

April 17, 18, 19
10:00 to 4:00
Corner of Grand and Main Street

Great Goodies

Lemonade + Cookies FOR SALE ➡

POSTERS

Posters are a great way to advertise your product. Your poster should include the name of the product and when and where people can buy it. Hang posters where a lot of people will see them. Be sure to ask permission before hanging a poster. Some places have bulletin boards where you can hang posters:

* apartment building lobbies
* stores
* community centers
* schools
* places of worship

SIGNS

If you are having a sale, make signs to advertise it. Write big! People should be able to read them from a distance. Draw arrows on the signs to lead people to the sale. Hang your signs where a lot of people will see them. You may need to ask permission before hanging them.

Make Your Own Poster

1 **Design** a **master** copy of your poster on a sheet of white paper.

2 Use bright colors so your poster will stand out. If you plan to use a black-and-white copier, use black on the master, and copy it onto colored paper.

3 Remember that copiers won't copy anything written too close to the edge of the master. So leave a border of at least ¼ inch (½ cm) on all sides.

4 Make as many copies of the master as you need. Then color in your posters!

WHAT YOU'LL NEED

white paper

black pen

ruler

copier

markers or colored pencils

colored paper (optional)

Money Matters

One reason you are selling something is to make money! Here are some hints about money.

THE BUDGET

First, figure out the expenses. List everything you have to buy in order to sell your product. Are you making the product? Include the supplies you need. Are you buying something to resell? Include the amount you paid for it. Don't forget costs such as advertising, signs, and packaging. Add up the amounts. These are your expenses.

Next, figure out the income. How much money do you think you can make selling your product? How many do you think you can sell? You should charge more than it cost you to make or buy the product. But you can't charge more than people think it's worth. If you set the price too high, people won't buy it.

Great Goodies Budget

EXPENSES

Lemonade ingredients	HAVE	BUY	ACTUAL
Water	X		
Lemons		$8.00	
Sugar		$5.00	
Snacks			
Cookies (store bought)		$6.00	
Supplies			
Lemon squeezer	X		
Ice		$5.00	
Pitcher	X		
Plastic glasses		$10.00	
Advertising			
Cardboard for sign	X		
Markers		$2.00	
Paint		$2.00	
Tape	X		
Copying the flyers		$4.00	
TOTAL EXPENSES		**$42.00**	

INCOME

		ACTUAL
Lemonade Sales 50 @ 1.00/each	$50.00	
Cookie Sales 20 @ .75/each	$15.00	
TOTAL INCOME	**$65.00**	

	ESTIMATE	ACTUAL
INCOME	$65.00	
LESS EXPENSES	-$42.00	
PROFIT	$23.00	

Sample form: make yours fit your business!

14

PROFIT OR LOSS?

If the income is more than the expenses, you will make a profit. If the expenses are more than the income, you will lose money selling your product.

Do you think you can make more money than you spend? You won't know for sure until you try. Start with just a few products and see how it goes.

If at first you don't make a profit, try to cut your expenses. If there is no way to do that, try another idea.

KEEPING RECORDS

In sales, it's especially important to keep complete records. Have a notebook for listing every single expense. Note the dates of your purchases and what products or sales they were used for.

Keep records of your income in a separate notebook. Write down what you sell, when, where, and for how much. Good record-keeping will help you figure out exactly how much you made or lost.

HANDLING MONEY

When you start selling your product, be ready to make change. Have extra five-dollar bills, one-dollar bills, and coins.

If someone gives you a large bill, leave it out while you count the change. That way you won't forget what bill you are making change for. Use a calculator to add up purchases.

It's a good idea to have a cash box with a lock on it. Someone should always be with the cash box. When you are done selling, put it in a safe place.

Presentation and Packaging

The appearance of your product should appeal to your customers. How you present a product can make a difference in your sales.

UNDERSTAND YOUR CUSTOMER

The packaging of your product should be appropriate for your customer. For example, products for kids should have bright colors. Writing on products for older people should be large and easy to read.

PROPS AND DECORATION

Make your "shop" **attractive** and interesting. Cover the table with a tablecloth. Think of things that go with your product. Display your product with them.

Look at displays at department stores and craft fairs. You can get good ideas for presenting your product.

WHAT'S YOUR BRAND?

Make your packaging an ad for your company. Be sure to put your company name on your packaging. Use the same colors and type or writing style each time. Maybe you could even create a logo. Soon people will begin to recognize your brand.

You could also include your phone number or e-mail address. Then customers can contact you if they want to buy more. Remember to ask your parent's permission before giving out your contact information.

SIGNS AND PRICING

Your signs should be easy to read and understand. They should tell your customers everything they need to know. Add pictures of people using your product. Customers will see how fun or useful it is.

Be sure that the price is clearly visible. People shouldn't have to ask how much something costs. Consider offering a **discount** if people buy more than one of something.

UNDERSTAND YOUR PRODUCT

What type of packaging suits your product? For example, baked goods should be packaged using food-safe **materials**.

PACKAGE LIKE THIS ☺

DON'T PACKAGE LIKE THIS ☹

Garage Sale Savvy

One way to make money selling things is to have a **garage sale**. You can sell things that you are no longer using. One person's trash can be another person's treasure! Since you already have the products, you won't have many expenses.

BEFORE YOU BEGIN

Before you have a **garage sale**, you need permission from your parents. Or maybe your parents are already planning a sale. Ask if you can set up a separate table for your stuff.

Ask if it's okay to sell the things you want to sell. Do they belong to you? Are they things that another family member may need or want?

Clean everything you are selling. Make sure the pockets of any clothes are empty.

Mark everything with a price. The prices should be clearly marked. Get a cash box and some change.

Cover up or block off areas where there are things that are not for sale.

Save newspapers to wrap any breakable things in. Save shopping bags for your customers to use.

Use cards and signs to advertise the sale (see pages 10–13).

SALE TIPS

* Are you are selling with other people? Mark each price sticker with the name of its seller. Take the stickers off of things that you sell. Keep the stickers so you know how much money each person gets.

* Play some background music. Choose music that most people enjoy. Don't play it too loud.

* Display things so they can be seen easily. Put things that are similar near each other. Don't just set out boxes of stuff. If you are selling books, make sure the spines show. Clothing looks better on hangers than in a pile.

* Make sure someone is always watching the cash box.

* Check at the library or online for more garage sale tips. You can learn more about having a successful sale.

DONATE
If there are things that don't sell, give them to a charity.

Crafty Art Sale

Are you creative? Do you love to make stuff? If so, there might be a market for your arts and crafts!

RECYCLE!
Check around your house for materials that you can recycle in your art projects!

BEFORE YOU BEGIN

There is more to selling your art than just making cool stuff.

Ask your friends and relatives whether they think your art will sell. Get more market **research** ideas on pages 6–7.

There are questions to think about when you set your prices. What did the **materials** cost? How much time did it take you to make each piece? What are your other expenses? How much will people pay for your art?

What kind of packaging will you need? Is your art breakable? Will you need to wrap it in newspaper? Does it need a bag or a box?

Do you want to have labels or tags with your business name on them? How about business cards to hand out? See pages 10–13 for information about advertising and presentation.

SALES TIPS

* Be sure each product is labeled clearly with its price.

* Keep your display simple and **attractive**. Take time between sales to clean up your table.

* Set out a bowl of candy or other free treat. It will draw people to your sale.

  If possible, show the customers how you make your art. That way they can see how much work it takes to create each piece.

* Dress neatly and be friendly to your customers. Smile and talk to people, but don't pressure them to buy something.

* Bring along tools that you might need to fix a piece if it gets broken.

* Keep a record of what sells well. Then you will know what to make for the next sale.

CRAFTY IDEAS

Here are some ideas for art and craft products to make and sell. Look at the library or online for other cool ideas.

JEWELRY

There are endless types of **jewelry** you can create. You can string beads to make lovely necklaces or bracelets. You can even make your own beads out of polymer clay. There are some very creative things you can do with buttons. And you can decorate barrettes with glue-on jewels and glitter glue.

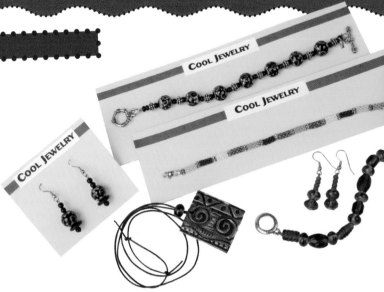

HANDMADE SOAP

With melt-and-pour soap, you can make many kinds of wonderful soaps. Use different molds, colors, and scents. The library, the Internet, and craft stores will have other soap-making ideas. Package your soaps in fabric, paper, or plastic bags. Tie ribbons around them for decoration.

PAPER CRAFTS

If you like to cut, paste, rubber-stamp, and draw, paper could be your thing. There is so much you can do with paper. For example, try making fancy or funny greeting cards. You can buy envelopes for them at craft or paper stores. **Design** your own giftwrap for different occasions. Make fun magnets from your own art or pictures from magazines. Use parts of pictures to make special bookmarks.

PAINTED STUFF

Decorated objects are great for personal use or as gifts. Buy unpainted wood objects at a craft store. They'll have things such as small boxes, picture frames, or candlesticks. Create your **designs** with paintbrushes, sponges, rubber stamps, or stencils. Wait for the paint or ink to dry. Then add finishing touches, such as glue-on jewels or glitter glue.

23

Great Goodies

You can never go wrong with selling snacks and baked goods! People love to treat themselves. And special foods make great gifts.

Great Goodies

Great Goodies

BEFORE YOU BEGIN

Decide what to buy or make for your sale. Try some popular favorites or create your own recipe!

Try to pick a location where a lot of people will be. It could be a neighborhood **garage sale** or other event. Be sure to get permission to set up shop.

Buy large bags of snacks at a store. Look for things that are on sale. Try trail mix, popcorn, or chips. Divide the snacks into zippered sandwich bags for selling. Create **attractive** packaging for your products. See pages 16–17 for ideas.

Add up your expenses and divide by the number of products. That is how much each one cost you. You need to charge a little more than that to make a profit. See pages 14–15 for tips on creating a budget.

Use cards and signs to advertise the sale (see pages 10–13).

REINVEST
Use some of your profit to buy supplies for your next sale.

SALE TIPS

* Decorate your stand so the food and drinks look their best!

* The prices should be visible and easy to read.

* Have cups, napkins, plates, or whatever else people need to enjoy the goodies. Don't forget to include these things in your expenses.

FOOD SAFETY

* You must pay special attention to cleanliness when making and packaging food. Have an adult **research** any special rules about selling food in your area.

* An adult should be present when you prepare and package your food products.

* If you have long hair, tie it back or wear a cap.

* Wash your hands with soap and hot water before you begin. Keep your work area very clean while you are handling food.

There are many kinds of goodies you can sell. The sky is the limit! Try some of these ideas to get you started!

LEMONADE AND COOL DRINKS

There's nothing better than a cool drink on a hot day! The hotter it is, the better your business could be.

You can make your own lemonade or buy soda and bottled water to resell. Keep the drinks in a cooler with a lot of ice so they stay cold.

Try setting up near a running or biking path. Make sure you have permission wherever you set up shop.

RECIPE IN A JAR

Put the dry ingredients for recipes in jars. Decorate the jars any way you like. Cut out circles of fabric. Wrap them over the lids and tie them on with ribbons. Tie a card to each one that explains how to prepare the recipe. There are many types of recipes you can try, including:

* cocoa mix
* bean soup mix
* brownie mix
* muffin mix
* bread mix
* cookie mix

BAKED GOODS

If you like to bake, try making some cookies, cupcakes, or brownies. Decorate them in creative ways. Or, you could bake bread or muffins.

Wrap the products individually to sell. Try adding some ribbon, or maybe a label with your company name on it!

Have some boxes or bags on hand. Then people can buy a bunch!

SWEET SPOONS

Here's a sweet idea for making special spoons for stirring coffee or cocoa. They are great to give as gifts. Melt some white chocolate, milk chocolate, or dark chocolate. Dip sturdy plastic spoons into the chocolate. Cover the entire bowl of each spoon. Place the dipped spoons on a cookie sheet covered with wax paper. Let the chocolate cool completely. Wrap the spoons in plastic and tie ribbons around them.

Try decorating the spoons. Before the chocolate cools, put candy sprinkles on them. Or after the chocolate cools, paint them with another color of chocolate. You could draw letters or pretty **designs**. Let the designs cool before wrapping the spoons.

Homegrown Garden Goods

Do you like plants and gardening? Try growing vegetables, **herbs**, or flowers to sell. You could also sell seeds or seedlings.

Think about who your customers are. What plants are popular in your area?

Learn about the best ways to grow high quality plants. If your produce is fresh and healthy, your sales will be better.

Many **perennials** need to be divided. When you divide them, you'll have extra plants you can sell!

Decide where to sell your garden goods. You could set up a stand in your yard. Or contact your local farmer's market for information about selling there.

When you can sell garden goods depends on the season. Sell seedlings in the spring when people start to plant their own gardens. Sell garden produce in the summer and fall when it is ripe.

Visit a farmer's market and see how others show their produce.

Use cards and signs to advertise the sale (see pages 10–13).

SALE TIPS

* Wash and arrange your produce so it looks pleasing. Group vegetables and flowers by color. Produce will stay fresher if it is kept in the shade.

* Watch the weather forecast. You'll get more customers on a sunny day!

* Make sure your prices are clearly marked.

* Give customers information sheets about the plant or produce they bought.

* Hand out recipes that use the produce you are selling.

* **Research** at the library or online how to grow and sell produce.

Tips for Success

Success isn't measured just by how much money you make on a sales event. How the event turned out is also important. Did the people who came like what you were selling? Will they buy at other events you organize?

PLAN, PLAN, PLAN

Planning is the most important part of starting a sales business. Plan every **detail** of your sale, from what to sell to what to do with the profits.

BE DEPENDABLE

Complete any task you agree to do on time. The sale will only be a success if everyone does his or her part.

BE ON THE SAFE SIDE

Follow safety instructions. Make sure all areas of your sale are safe.

BE POLITE

Respect your customers. Be friendly and thank people for coming to your sale. Be respectful even if you don't agree with someone.

REVIEW

After the sale, review how it went. What sold well? What didn't? What would make your business more profitable? Take notes to use when planning your next sale.

THIS IS JUST THE BEGINNING

Okay, it is the end of the book. But, it is just the beginning for you! This book has provided information about some ways to make money. Now decide what might work for you. Talk it over with your parents. And don't forget to have fun!

Glossary

attract – to cause someone or something to come near. If something is *attractive*, it is pleasing to look at and be near.

competition – other individuals or groups wanting the same thing.

design – 1. a decorative pattern or arrangement. 2. to create something based on your own plan.

detail – a small part of something.

discount – an amount taken off of the price of something.

garage sale – a sale that takes place in a garage.

herb – a scented plant used to flavor food or make medicine.

master – an original copy that is reproduced to make more of the same thing.

material – the substance something is made of, such as metal, fabric, or plastic.

perennial – a plant that grows back every year.

research – 1. the study of something to learn new information. 2. to find out more about something.

schedule – a list of the times when things will happen.

volunteer – to offer to do a job, most often without pay.

WEB SITES

To learn more about the jobs that kids can do, visit ABDO Publishing Company on the World Wide Web at www.abdopublishing.com. Web sites about creative ways for kids to earn money are featured on our Book Links page. These links are routinely monitored and updated to provide the most current information available.

Index